*This in Words,
For Reverence of
Wonder...*

This in Words, For Reverence of Wonder...

~ Philip Holland ~

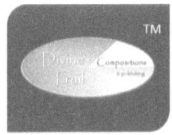

Dedicated to…
My family,
And to every reader who embraces my work with appreciation.

My expression has always been meant for you.

This in Words,
For Reverence of Wonder...

Contents

A Poet's Opening Line

Uh… Some folks say I may be a poet. Could you consider it?

So I've taken pen to compose in convincing prose deliberate!

This, although, is not the poem…

But I do have one in particular, and hope so much to recite it now,

If, perhaps, you might allow…

Me!

Sacred Moment Afire

When there is no effective solution,
False hope, woven and hung at the doorway
Between the warm interior and the cold desolation,
Will but slightly push away the ensuing, frightful night.

Be there ready while the firelight flames draw down to flickers;
Let loose the future's undisclosed answers,
Ready instead to grip mightily this immeasurable moment burning.
Stay with the moment, eyes upon whatever glow may be granted,
Radiating with life yet from the dying flicker.
Cherish this in its continuance of undiscovered years or days
Or seconds, if only.

Embodied in this – the living moment,
You wick a super-conscious, persistent fuel…
Hold fast to its undying eternity.
Indwell this tremendous instance, immediate with sublime wonders
Of colors, the textures, and of sounds still surrounding.
Turn fearful shivers into calm warmth for priceless memories
Drawn up from deepest reservoir of unbounded heart;
Your sentience express with gratitude
And brave faith for deliverance.
Be in love for living out all radiance to transpire
In this one moment's fire; come of it what may, for joy or despair.

Sing in harmony
With this eternal parlance of timeless and tranquil lyric,
Even so as hope for answers resolves into unknown ash.
Celebrate throughout
To wherever its cooling, thermal plume may carry you
As a final shimmering, fleeting ember.

Tiny Sailboats

Tiny sailboats drift away upon foamy, floating cradles
Set loose beyond the beach,
Her dearest love cast aloft in heartbeats mixed into the wind,
Thrusting along the tiny sails of each.
"Safest journeys," she prays them farewell,
Her tiny boats to ride out each swell,
Swiftly then by her breath of wishes mixed with the wind
Until anchors fall in the home ports at journey's end,
To at last deliver sweet fruits from every hold,
Her sad, sweet love carried home to friends of old...

A Paragon as Only You May Dramatize

Residing – a turning; a full rendition from curtains drawn open,
Until drawn to a close.
A paragon takes stage,
For each who is born, and for you,
As only each may uniquely dramatize
From sole character and from sole conception.
In this exclusivity – your time of anatomic, autonomic,
Rhythmic lust –
Inhale and exhale, soldiering forward two by two.
Squeeze the gentle metronomic myocardium
For rush of want by inner streams of thirsty blue.
A paragon of one essence true,
A want of one continuance, upon the stage but once…

Pray your life with pastels flicked to spatter against
A translucent canvas,
Wet specks and hatched strokes into needful patterns of
Your special life's groans and gratitude;
All of them dreamt to be traced upon the watchful eyes
Of your contrived, perfect acrylic Lord.

Prepare to believe by what dimensions you inhabit,
You transcend, you transmute.
Perspire by ardent resolution for every refraction
You alone conceive,
Bear witness and beset your demise from allegiance to
One unicorn rare,
One sole, individual heart with only your impossible perception.
Ride aloft, and ride far,
Until the impossible beast – the irreplaceable human –
Prolongs no more.

4

Social Media Censored the Visual Metaphor

I cannot use the visual metaphor here on Social Media anymore,
Because they come for me to censor what I create for you to see…

If I attempt to warn,
Hoping to remind,
Hard truth is a misery we deny
By pretense of delusion while we divide.

And thus once again regrouping into warring camps,
We will return as animals
To finally rage and to bash one another's skulls,
After the fools are allowed repeatedly to rule,
Pushing hell's madness across this place of heaven.

I tried to show you the historical faces,
The rot of crushed humans laid down in War's ugly spaces.
But you know better than I.
You always know better than I do.

I cannot use the visual metaphor here on Social Media anymore,
Because they come for me to censor what I create for you to see…

Inner Embrace

Walk with me
When thee in devastation, trembles
Breach with me
When thee in deprivation, grapples
Hope with me
When thee in mortal trial, falters
Take of my breath
When thou hast winded.
Revive in my strength
When thou hast exhausted.
Rejoice with me
When thee in desperate prayers, profess.

And still if thee believeth not
My omnipotence present,
Then look for me within thine own eyes,
Embrace me within thine own heartbeat,
Until that which thou grievously suffers, withers overcome
And we are held in one together;

With thee beholding thine confidence in powerful patrimony,
Allowing it forever thus.

One Thing – You and Me

At one thousand miles per hour,
Standing together in near proximity,
We are spinning through day and night – you and me.
At sixty seven thousand miles per hour,
Together we take another run around our glorious sun.
We call this particular moment "2018."

Although we are indifferent to shared glances,
Side-stepping with parting ways
As strangers beyond brief exchanges,
We are choreographing together, this reality upholding,
This reality unfolding.

"By what meaning, and for what purpose?"
We ask against the uncertainty?

…While the star burns away a bit more hydrogen,
Uncertainty fills with today's story expressed
From us together, through which we do define the unanswered.
ONE THING – you and me.

Quietly, the Rain Falls for Beth Vilomah

From the cold air way high,
Downward a silent driblet falls,
A cool crystalline tiny orb,
Delicate, clear pearl racing loose,
Hidden in a dash velocity,
Sent hurling for witness but briefly,
And plunged to a final bursting splash;
Whispering of abrupt collision,
Blasting apart with a quiet patter.

To its precipitous ending, in echo a billion faintly splatters;
This silvery drizzling,
To hem a skyward drapery of endless descending pearls.
A sea of streaming droplets splashing in soothing cadence
There for me, to calm my weepy heart;
Wherein the shushing rain anoints my burden
And sets me temporarily to wash clean a troublesome stain.
Serenely, beneath the shimmering mist,
I resonate to the light of rainbows.

Inside a Master's Paradox, Come to Hold Me Now

Here in this life's grandeur,
From heartbeats to brightly burning galaxies,
In the immensity between and beyond these two,
A paradox is the Lord's busy hand.

Each night for its draining vacuum,
Each day for its annealing forge,
Overbearing a blind, stumbling world,
What of this life defines us?
But the Master's thrust
To display us all in paradox.

Persevere as we do,
I lament to finally love you!
You dream thirsty for love,
And to express love too, surely,
While the high resonant harmony
Entwined with the low degenerative disorder
Takes hold the world's unsteady affair,
Choosing to marry delightful wonder
Banded together with grievous disrepair.

And I always ache to hold you,
As you may for the same embraces tightly,
That we might, in our clutching protection,
Feel safely secure
Apart this vast churning volition residing.

Barbara

Sweet, mythical mysteries...
Who will she know to trust, to guide her?
And where may she trust enough to follow?
Where she goes now, as she may,
To follow worries and fears down the dark alleys bending,
Unending, one to another.
So she seeks out a savior's daylight
Between all these dread alleyways...

All but the sweet mysteries,
Confound her troubled wonder.

He sees the sweet mysteries
All fallen away,
Her brunette heart in animate charms,
This only, upon his eyes.
All the sparkle she displays
Addressed to him through soft, imbuing hands;
To remind him, a woman's powerful mystique...
With all her sensual affect upon him.

He sees,
He feels so deeply,
Though he forsakes
What firm love yearns mortal-bound devotedly;
For blinded as he may be of mythical faith,
She indwells there with deep belief, these sweet mysteries
Upon her head, upon her mind, all through her heart.
She climbs the stairs to higher alters,
She prays a marriage to the one intangible husband
Whom holds together her onerous world...

He sees the sweet mythical mysteries
All fallen away,
Her presence alight, rich and sultry,
This only, mirage before his thirsty, desert eyes.
Her effervescence born twinkling aglow with lightest hazels
Race a crush all through, she places there by touch of soft imbuing;
To remind him, a woman's powerful mystique…
With all her sensual affect upon him.

Metaphysics 28

I may, with my thoughts...
Resonant vibrations victorious against conditions notwithstanding,
Powerful, subtle waves!
Potentiality to wash you warm and clean,
As I have seen you there all along!

My Friends, My Protectors, My Soldiers

Are each of us the fool?
Ignorant to the sacrifices.
Would I risk my merry delight of fingers?
Risk my eyes, my legs, expose my youthful wholeness
To suffer forward a life of partial creature?

What young man or woman moves forward today
That I damn to unknown consequences awaiting them?
Just as water pure runs the terrible, deep troughs to sustain me,
So my soldiers have crossed the seconds, minutes,
Hours and days terrified,
For services of agony, sacrifices of soul,
Mortal loss of all they hold dear.

But we fools will never know them.
We did not join them beside the grave's ledge.
We did not slightly behold it,
Nor share in freedom's costly nightmare:
The immediate fracture upon their soul
By fear's thundering hammer.

We are so foolish that we may never fully understand the gravity,
The delicacy, this peaceful gift of life with its safety and its free joy
Of which my soldiers bring back quietly from the blackest storms,
To place such hallowed gift following me intimately from behind,
As a shadow for which I give such thoughtless regard.

I am indeed a fool to ever forget them:
My friends,
My protectors,
My soldiers…

Gentle Thomas Over There

He waits for you,
Waits as your friendly lad in a small ball cap,
As your young sailor o'er sea,
As your intrepid partner once prime,
As your discordant, impatient, virile male;
Evermore the gentle white soul in brittle, old bone
But powerfully in love with you.

Oh yes,
He waits in his soft song sung along a breeze,
Waiting in a pale, cool morning,
Waiting in reverent radiance as the late hour
On a summer's steamy day.

Yes, waiting beside your quiet reminiscence
Of time rolling past into gloss and joyous shimmer.
He is waiting to wash you over with diamond light,
Born ahead into perfect being at the midnight
Of a long day's walk with you.

What So Sweet As Love?

What so sweet as Love?
What so potent as Love?
Whatever Love, what gift but Love?
No other like Love.

And what proof of Love?
Love's trace in every feeling, infused through every healing,
Incites each spirited passion,
Undulates through venous flows to oceans' fathom,
Resonates as starlight and universal dominion.

Finally beholding to its proof – Love as life's dominant truth,
Our deep yearning to know it more...

"Theybies," Ken Dolls and Barbie Dolls

When I was three, I had to tinkle dee
And I noticed my pee was in an arching stream
Not a downward dribble,
Oh my, I thought, what a riddle!

Because at two, there wasn't much to do
But enjoy the warm, wet wrap around my middle.

Now at four, there seems to be something more
To this riddle of stream and dribble…
Time to set aside these parts of which I was born,
These parts are not the "me" in Mommy's and Daddy's "Theyby,"
I can choose to call me "he" or call me "she"
Because the dribble and the stream won't mean a thing
In my elastic mind of powerful delusion!

At five I will march brightly alive
Ready for this world Mom and Dad have made,
Blue can be green! And red instead can be yellow too!
It will all have nothing to do with anything
But what my little mind believes true!
And whoever can't agree…
Will simply not belong
In my little world that is perfectly right for me!

8:28 Rendered

I accept that I am the living fortune,
As I have been seen
In all that I am blessed to enfold
By the infinite Lord's perfect dream
Upon me.

I trust with each faith-filled step
That I am delivered sweetly,
Along beside this merciful guiding light.

As eternity and expression braid
To reveal Love's great purpose,
I witness now in honor thereof,
While I celebrate for tomorrow's great bounty.

Unicorn

Polyamory, which haunts her…
Or drives her as a deeply persistent pulse...
Or is it this woman's wildness powerful – rare in depth of craving,
Rare in generosity to share herself eagerly;
She clutches a loving bond through emotions devoted,
But dares departing it serenely,
And without thought or greed of possessive scorn.
A ménage she promotes as doting mistress to wedded darlings,
For thrice so powerful the monogamous, conventional union
– pairing moonstruck lovers.
A Troika of sincerest pansexual magnificence,
These affairs deepen, all the while unpossessed.

Orgiastic paramours consummate their conjugal rapture within her.
She responds upon them with incomparable, connubial passion
For her triune romance.
Avowing her bareness in fruits of lust and love,
Darlings three, partake a communing,
Kisses and gazes, caresses and tastes,
Unicorn feasting upon all their pleasance of delicious flavors:
Softly pear, firmly apple, lush juices in velvety peach.

Yes, she moves with strides so unconstrained!
And thereby this pansexual gallops freely!
Lesbian betrothal in tender lust through unbridled affair
Of feminine intensity.

She nuzzles to take hold, she seduces to let go
Enchantress with ease, her suiters both male and female.
She sips from each of them,
Their bodies and their ardent temperaments!

18

No man rises so rare a Dionysian,
As to compare her impassioned, fervid Unicorn.
The masculine steed is born more bedeviled
In homophobic conformity,
Prisoner corralled to a harsher, judgmental world
Shall he remain bridled;
Save for his frustrated, narrowly concealed, unbridled soul…

Not verily born for conforming, our unicorn mare;
She sprints from low, vanilla valleys
Racing higher to capsicum plateaus,
Swift and beautiful – the leaping unicorn,
She vaults a restraining prickly hedgerow,
O'er to plush meadows of mythical, tremendous romance.

Ardent and Nuclear Purpose

What canst thou? If not forever with me, my only maiden,
Sweetly sworn to become us
As ours' of perfect valence in steep enrapture…

Time and space waste if no promise will fulfill it,
If not but to find you, to feel you,
To entwine we two,
Invest of our hands and our hearts
Through ardent and nuclear purpose.

Ultima Thule, I Perceive New Horizons Truly
- Arrokoth

Ultima Thule,
Beside your limits I perceive this truly,
Four billion, ninety three million miles
Removed from everyone.

Adrift mere strands of photon quanta,
Far behind the bleeding Sun,
I breach passed you in the crushing blackness
Along severest solitude toward my empty mission done.

Ultima Thule,
I arrive by thrust of lonesome duty,
I'm outcast into the frozen wonders,
I drift in absence from sisters and my brothers.

I've no remorse, my far flung course to divorce me
My native world – locked in delusive orbit back there.
In its sprawl of tumultuous mortal features
From ragged shores to lightest air,
Homo genus retaliates where subordination embroils
Upon lore and myth for Godly covenants or other lies,
Entanglements expressed epic, across History's foibles.

Instead,
Slowly away four billions past Mother's nervous planet,
I rush nearby your remotest silent axis;
On course for what unearthly in vast and grander beauty,
Ultima Thule.

I Am Wicked in My United States Citizenship

I am a wicked man they tell me
For what I choose to believe:
My pride in Country, to guard it heavily at the perimeter,
A vigilance at the window,
At every door to establish firmly the home within.
My wicked pride to stand beside this U.S. Constitution,
To attest that my Forefathers' Constitution is best, better in its ideals
Of liberty and freedom and equality;
Better than any other in its responsible edicts
To protect and to serve the homeland,
To adjudicate a just and lawful society.
Better than every Constitution yet known historically
To set the ways and behaviors of humans.
Yes, I am this wicked to assert my pride and set first a table
For this exclusive society vetted to be
Its lawful, law-abiding citizens.
Protect the windows and bar the doors
While my fellow countrywomen and countrymen
Feast in bounty harvested from wild, American ingenuity.

There will always be marauders at the gates,
And I am wicked enough to believe in
Mighty protection against them.
By the precepts of this U.S. Constitution,
A world is learning to emulate its art in liberty and freedom.
As I will wickedly choose to stand in strength at every post,
The art of tyranny takes notice;
A weaker Country shall be opposed,
As history of human carnage shows.

And the less fortunate worlds are not forsaken,
Not directly taken to ground by these United States,
The imperfect world knows better that this Country
Has made more of compassion than any before.

Owing much to men and women who have sacrificed limb and life
On distant shore,
A respectful memorial to honor them
With prudent locks upon the door,
I state loudly my firm "Yes," to protect these treasures
Of Constitution, culture, and commerce.
Best that you not tread, sour citizen, for I do wish you worse
Wishing you there, in some other "perfect place" to abide,
Until you reclaim a proper U.S. pride.

Yes, I am a guilty man, as accused by the self-loathing haters,
Guilty to believe and stand beside the wisdom of our framers,
Guilty for my pride in Country, and to protect it heavily,
Guilty to rise above this struggling world,
Announcing my United States citizenship merrily!

Undoing, By the Silence of Unspoken Tremors

What furtive doubt is this that thou casts repeatedly before me?
Thine vague silence nondescript, spares me no further,
Which by honest words discriminately spoken could at least attest
With poignant clarity.

I would choose the directly spoken wounding better,
For sooner its purposeful amputation and healing done.
Thine complacency for this and for that of naked authenticity,
Deferred always in silent tremor,
Makes for a rapier of slow laceration upon me;
Wouldst that I will hemorrhage insecurities worse
For ill confidence of what we strain in resolve between us.

But I do understand you, for I too cannot speak of it.
I call out quietly from a dark closet,
Forever intending to speak my genuine voice.
Silence, or the congenial shallows
Are my safest spaces beside you, my Love…
Upon a time once,
We were madly, gladly together as two engaging voices.
What must we speak in feelings before this ending,
To lead us again?
Saved back to our talkative beginning.

Screwball Lord

Screwball Lord,
Spinning, hurling in waves of rays,
And sub-atomic strings vibrating into molecular beings,
Orbiting away with cosmic decay…

Vibrational dreams oscillating like wild cello strings,
With afflicted musicians possessed to emulate better than all,
Our screwball Lord –
Whom clangs out and jangles through,
Permeant this whole musical affair of sweet heaven and hell.
Loud drums of searing infernal destruction
Twined together with cooling flutes of quiet truce!

Can't Help but Adore

In streams of scenes, her silent beauty
Sets my eye to wonder,
No difficulty to dream the fantasy to gain,
To pair up into her heart,
To whisper her name…

My lips won't forget
The last time, the next time,
I'm caught up, my heart has purchased another golden string.

How am I to keep free, this lost in you?

Ways of Love, Autumn Gusts

In sweetest gifts, so these lips imparted between us
What the quiet heart could not rise to speak out...

Autumn gusts carry off ardent feelings unspoken,
A summer's splendor which failed to find its yield...
Surely lain there into the fields,
Latent seeds of a very special promise.
How I sadden to turn them under.
How will I learn to let you go?

Clouds

Comes a cloud tumbling,
Off horizons…
Soaring,
Slow,
Motion,
In shapes that never last.

See the cloud
Harnessed to no one,
White gypsy blossom,
Flowing forward
To leave us passed.

Run from the Collision

Come inside, there is no reason to hide.
Back again so soon? Of course you can!
Ignore the Racists in the basement who chased you out.
The Good People on the main floor leave wide an open door.
Whatever mess you make matters little more.
Claim the identity. Get smashing drunk and wreck the car.
Such messes are... No worse, the messiness
Displayed by our own insolent children – so what can we do?

Just run to hide again outside these walls,
Until we silence the blustery, Bigots wailing in the halls.
No need to hurry, don't you worry.
We will excuse you with our focus driven,
To applaud the little foreign woman cleaning in the kitchen.

Many of us inside believe ourselves compassionate
To look the other way,
We turn our heads from the messes you ran to deny yesterday.

Back again for the third, fourth, tenth time? Fine...
We have grown accustomed to our own family's constant feuding.
We hold that door for you wide,
While we roll our eyes at the family's chasm brewing.
You see, we think ourselves the pride of this neighborhood.
Stop hiding in the bushes and come back inside,
We think it's all good!

Todd Michael... October

There is a hole in the floor,
A round sort of tunnel which drops,
A hidden destination under the black empty center...

There are whispers which tap the attention of my recollection,
Taking me back to you.
Is it this warm, autumn day? Like it was then?
What makes crescendo of these oft undisturbed whispers?

I failed you...
I return to reclaim this, periodically.
I witnessed it there behind the darting of your eyes.
I may have reached you, there on the quiet bank,
Your very private bank along the muddled waters.
I heard it in your voice as we drank, as we became all too drunk.
You wanted to hail me a cab. You worried for me!
I was a miserable mess but so strong upon my thriving,
Denying wing.
I misread you there, with all my dismissive blind confidence,
I presumed the trouble
Was merely a hassle against your enviable mettle.
We exchanged the last subtle warnings in one last phone call,
Whispers thrown out to my deaf soul,
They did not alarm that this was my last chance to save you...

There is a hole in the floor,
A round sort of tunnel which drops,
A hidden destination under the black empty center...

There are whispers which tap the attention of my recollection,
Taking me back to you.
Is it this warm, autumn day? Like it was then?
What makes crescendo of these oft undisturbed whispers?
Not so many years yet have passed you by.
They have passed the "we" of us by,
Left with only undisturbed whispers…
You would have enjoyed this sunny, warm, autumn afternoon,
I would have enjoyed the voice of my friend.

Pariahs of the Wild Deep

A soaring giant stands throbbing in two tiny shoes,
Longing to merengue with dwarfish dancers prancing far below.
Entreating, gluttonous, flab femme splays and splinters
A temple's pew,
Squeezing cumbersome prayers between
Slender congregants' lighter few.

As with obtrusive giants, and ravenous gobblers obese,
Wild pariahs of the libidinous waters …alike.

Oh hallow the yearning, burning craving of my loins primeval!
But I am cajoled to betray my wild, this unbridled deep;
Admonished, that I must my weaning withdrawal,
For edicts evangelic
Or be cast out otherwise!

…As sinful pariahs will be chastised
By prim prima donnas – languid with hobbled appetites.

"Woke," To See the Neo-Fascist Ideal

I walk along, admiring myself as righteous,
Cuz I am "woke."
See myself to be superior morally,
Cuz I am "woke."

Judging you to blame,
Faulting you to shame,
By all your whiteness game,
Cuz I am "woke."

Betty June in Transcendence

Transcendent soul...
Our mother, she chooses carefully her thoughts,
Resolved to delight in peacefulness.

Oh! How she places her Lord highest;
Her Lord handsome with wisdom,
Charismatic inner sanctum that shows a finer focus
Beyond distraction.
She is ever devoted beside,
In love with her Lord's beauty and true transcendence.

How so in this woman's gentle frame, does she re-enforce
To bear up with girded constitution?
We cannot but admire her insistence,
That in each of her choices shall come first an affirmative prayer,
To receive life faithfully, with fortitudinous grace.

Elderly today, but still so youthful –
She strides a pace that keeps with or surpasses
Those of us younger.
What invigorates her so determinedly strong?
But the sureness of her conviction.

And I, the meeker soul born out,
I wander beside her,
Grateful to receive her cleansing blessing.

All that she aspires to become
Is astride a constant sense of spiritual determination.
She does not bewail the day's challenges
Rather, she adheres to a re-aligning law.
Her steadiness wills to control the thought, not the situation –
So proves her love for, her faith in the promise of mental healing.

Matriarch, once young dreamer of dances and ballet,
You have danced wonderfully before these children.
In each of your pirouettes lively,
You have taught another step toward perfection.

One sooner Chance, Rarest Special Presence

She cannot be so perfectly beautiful,
Woe the effect of her that I do recall,
As a butterfly that I loose from my window's ledge
Before I behold its rarest, special presence there.

She cannot have kissed me that deeply passionate
That I could now forget her;
She cannot in her sweet charms pervading,
Though as I must and do remember,
And I look back beyond all others,
Forgetting them not nearly so finally fairest.

She cannot make herself the reward
Unto another man,
I pray against such fate forever No!
While I desire,
By all intensity of equal hope,
And obsess to finally pull her closely to me
This one time more,
As one sooner sunrise might illuminate
Another promising daybreak of desperate chance,

That I could kneel to ask her,
My earnest courtship to allow;
While I am falling nearer to partake,
To embrace her delight,
Her highlight in all romance of my sincerest dreams.

Doers Good and Doers Evil

The essentially Divine rests within, alone,
While disgorging through mortal roles as doers good and doers evil.
All characters mortally played,
Eventually into dust are swept off stage.
Alone – Divinity eternal,
Portrays onward with boundless scenes of dramatic play...

My Vow, In This Thy Limbo

Oh, blissful Limbo…
I languish
While I meander upon silent beaches,
Salty scent of tranquil ebb and flow;
Let me go…
I can hold to the cold grip of anonymity.

In the numb Limbo…
Our day is wide between morning's light,
And night's sedate gloom;
Two doorways to every room,
Yet all is bare floor between the two.

Onto the indecisive Limbo…
Where the raw bone is made clean,
And a brittle leg breaks
To leave the Dreamer stranded
Aside the course-effort once taken to,
Once so quickly with a noble stride.
But now the stranded victim mills about.

To the aged Limbo…
Where old eyes look upon young figures
To lust the warm blood of heaven,
Where the sweet sculpture of soft, silken hair
Drapes and curls downward
Across the freshly youthful, sumptuous neckline;
Old hearts flutter to recall the essential healing
Inseminated from exuberant, palpable love.

Surely though, somewhere within me
God too infatuates in quietly desperate states
Of Limbo…
Coaxing my heartbeats between breath or grave,
Coercing my moments toward choices of gloom or of joy;
Suggesting between the two, a purpose
To believe, to celebrate, to cherish,
And to be, valiantly;
No matter what, this place of Limbo…

Perspective Isolated, in Monochrome Rainbows

Perspective...
Blank stare from the eyes,
Bump against walls blindly,
Licking clean – the cold, black slate board,
No matter a chalk full of lies.

Perspective...
Fasten attitude whereupon oblique impressions reign,
Gray matter concedes to dubious gray life.

Perspective...
Basis melts, continuity gone, clarity frosts cloudy.
Beneath this preeminent new rule,
No presumption fails, regardless false or true.

Perspective...
Poorer, the older order of set principles.
Paint the world ostensibly warmer now
But by sacrifice of necessary balance in contrast and form;
For what but to mollify the lousy craft of every bad artist
Who cannot perceive correct dimension
From the fruit and the bowl.

Wash this canvas blood red now,
Portray a difficult winter's twilight horizon – bitter, flat, and finite.
Some of us color-blind will still not receive it,
Still claiming to see it a cryptic refraction
Of monochrome rainbows...

One Thread to Follow You

What thread takes me to you?
Windswept, this life and loving within it,
Drifting by, this will not lend me to hold you
As I would choose to hold you closely forever.

What thread unseen?
Though mighty enough beyond this life,
Will promise me to bind us,
By one thread only, to follow you?
Or no...

Windswept, this life and loving within it,
This cannot be...
One delicate thread remaining I pray to seek,
To the mighty wind I commend my needful hope
The thread for all is finally love,
Love returning through each ending drifting by.

Beginning again, go around again,
Windswept along with you...

Sleek Irish Girl

You are so beautiful...
You make me conjure dreams for tomorrow...

I move into an imaginary web where
You have spun a sticky intent to desire me.

All your womanhood comes to bear,
While I inhale the perfume signature of a new day,
A wonderful play of all your lovingness for me.
I rave, "She wants me, she wants me...
She cannot help but fall into me."

So the day has come that my one lonesome heart
Beats stronger in the fullness of two, me with you.
Nothing matters like me with you.
Everything else is a false play.
We are the fresh nucleus of a long sought passion...
So we coalesce in a slow spin,
Like two slow rivers converging,
While here in the center, your close lips
Melt the vast world away,
To replace it all with a timeless moment in heaven.

I become a man again,
A man with the love she gives,
Like oxygen for the newborn.
All I see is your heart given upon my hand;
Suddenly I am not dying any longer.
I am repaired,
I am gently lowered to the soft white sand.
I press in tightly to the scent of your draping hair.

I cuddle sleeplessly for the healing balm
Of your warm, living being…

Then I cannot help but collapse inside your essence.
I drop serenity pebbles into a wide, deep pool
Immense in its fathom of all my pertinence of sentience;
Of all my thirst for being alive in love...
I raise my lips to your precious, delicate brow
For the touch of soft kisses endless.

Yes, I dream to be the weave of your silken desire...
I do pray to lie beside you,
Finally home with you, so willing to be with me so completely.

Bouquet of Tiny Lavender

Thought to be a boy who dared a bouquet of tiny lavender,
Passed a pink string from his pocket of jingling things
And placed it sheepishly into her lovely, soft palm.
June eyes of young glass where the puppy patters pass,
And tiny lavender bids forward his shy praise for her.

Charmed to be a girl free in every young thrill
For tiny lavender,
Bashful in a long, smooth braid tied in a big bow of blue
Painted up with rosy, blushing smiles too.
June eyes embrace with merry hush,
Two young hearts bind together in a pink springtime crush,
And tiny lavender bids forward a perfect day, forever…

So Much, the Necessity of You

So much,
So necessary for the day to become
All that it wondrously might,
...Relies on the necessity of expressing the wonderful you.

Don't doubt it.
Don't question it.
You are that essential card in a house of infinite cards –
By the tiniest of your intentions, the tiniest of your gestures,
By the most subtle of your deepest vibrations.

Without the magnitude of your unique being and becoming,
The wholeness of this ultimate house in its eternal day
Unravels as incompletely defined.

Think on most high, the special quality of the extraordinary you!

My Earthly America, 2018

Screaming, I fall off this day's hot ledge…

Human pain,
Where the gazelles leap from the lions,
Where the broiling desert sands sink while scorpions scamper clear.

Human fear,
Where the burning winds forsake a supple flower's thirsty petals,
Where baby rabbits rush in dread from diving eagles.

Human hate,
Where the rising Omega
Trains in oppressive ways against the dying Alpha,
Where the blind preach blindness
To the myopic eyes of their children…

Pansexual

If I am water, what of me then?
For in my purity I am here to blend within, to mix within.
Essentially undefined, I am born to become all things,
Tethered to no boundaries, I am water flowing.

There is no partnership in solution to which I cannot conform,
For I am water.
There is no earthen clay which will not embrace me,
I make no fight to resist my submission into mud,
No toxicant, no purulent, no fatal poison that I would deny
To save me from reviled certainty;
For I am always distilled clean in the end.
I am the enfolded solvent into all ambition expressed.

My nature roams with the destinies belonging to all others,
As I am by my absence of definition, so defined.
Remarkably, I am graced the pure!
Because I am water…

To Set Us Free, Wherefore this Uncertainty?

Sometimes I break down in a hurt of tears,
Because I couldn't save you.
Sometimes I just sit and cry for all my failure,
That I could not deliver your dreams.

In pain, for pity or for love?
I worry that I cannot distinguish between the two.
What if love? Then we could have made a mend,
Putting us back to the path again.
But pity could masquerade, and mend it wrong,
Never then could we live a lie for long.

This is how I worry for you,
I think of all the stealing storms that you have weathered;
The little, happy girl who wants just to play,
A jolly frolic in fields of sunflowers and rainbows rising!
You look for a day that comes to set you free from…
All those lonesome losses.

My feelings for you were real enough,
As my present, lingering pain will testify.
I became one more promising wing that could not fly,
Could not carry you to the golden leaves.

But I remember you more…
I will always remember you more…
I will always cherish you more…
Then I wonder, I worry,
Who of unknown companions yet will let me keep you near?
Into the end as my dearly, dearly loved friend.

Do not – with old pain carry – for one more new day,
And as well also for all days which may then follow!
Press on to breathe for greater good - all the wonders,
In laughter or in tears;
Because who or what force of fate stands able
For you or her or him or me,
To set us free from uncertain lives?

Ways of Love, a Monday's Sunrise

With a light skip, she arrives…
She's the springtime beauty,
Sweet enough to steal away any man's desire!
I pause my long, uncertain journey;
Let loose my baggage to imagine, to admire
A possible good day's tranquility in love…

I recall her within my growing sentiment,
While I consider what splendid petals she might arise to bloom,
For flower of friendly fondness and romantic possibilities to come.

A Night of Birth, Melody Girl

In a cool, quiet autumn night,
Beneath a serene dream of guiding moonlight,
I did rush to meet my beloved second daughter to be born.

In that sweet harvest of October,
Grace fell upon me to behold her,
And as a momentous Led Zeppelin sang a perfect invocation
To ramble on,
A baby girl came with her own inspired song
As a soul of perfect Melody.

Journey Forward

Sometimes off the lips,
Beneath polite, lingering phrases,
A hopeful metaphor rises up silently;
Inscribed between two pleasurable smiles exchanged.

As two may arrive in duet or may by solos depart,
Dance this journey forward,
Brave mariner, sailing your romantic heart...

Baby Anya

Dear Mother, Father,
I have known the best of Human experience.
My birth, my life, my family –
In each my heart held witness to your adoring gaze.
While mother cradled me, nursing me,
I slumbered… to behold that newly born serenity.
Mother, Father, I felt your praise
In every soft, gentle kiss.
My world was only love, love, love…

I am an Angel once more,
And I am now the purest of human soul…
Born in the life of God's most precious design,
Fulfilled with the blessing of whole innocence.

Dear Mother, Father,
Take heart that all of Time passes in illusion,
And I am complete now
In the timeless light of love with you.

DeAnne, Art, and Romantic Vintage

You are the precious destination that will not come to be,
Where this weary, sleeping traveler portrays his romance
Through nighttime's best dreams to see;
And each morning starting out again,
Prays my heart's starvation for that day's sweetest fruition…
Finally won,
Finally home to thrive in praise from
Your most beautiful and loving eyes.

Within and of Worlds Greater, and Farther Beyond!

Aggregate bounties embody, mind, and breath,
Charmed with animate endowment overwhelming,
Overflowing, overjoyed!
Singing within me these galaxies chiming,
Vast enumerative of trilling electrons, protons, neutrons
Personate in accord with deep insistent blessings…

I cannot seep this bursting outpour
Of all my gladdest tears…

I am, thank you!
I am, thank you!
I am, in greater dimension,
I am, within and of worlds greater, and farther beyond!

I am the lush, rushing and billowing iridescent white cumulus
Ascending mightily.
I cannot but behold the wonder of my own heart,
Magnificent in holy depth broader than
The grandest, old and open sky!

I too, thank you!
I too, thank you!
I do through and through in greater dimension,
I am, within and of worlds greater, and farther beyond!
By the day and the night of each breath,
Willing upon me all miracle, enigmatic!

Propensity Calls Me There

Am I a spider's thread, spun to vibrate aloft the passing wind?
Will I break, should I make my supple nature forcibly rigid?

Am I a crystal flake that forms and drifts
Along a swirling column of frigid air?
Can I hope to hold this crystalline form in hotter, tepid worlds?

Am I a swelling blossom,
Bursting to erupt in glorious beauty against the April light?
Will I wither, should I hold tightly closed?

Am I a healthy child as I cry and dance and sing,
Keeping busy with pretense and play?
What sad adult might I become
If my inner-child is bleak and sorrowfully grown?

Am I a masculine beast, haunted to perpetuate the ancestral tribe?
Will I starve in barren, lonesome ways
If I detach from patriarchal rhythms?

Finally, am I a man ultimately complete only once possessed
By a woman's love?
Can I survive if I choose otherwise but to abide
The course of this needful propensity?

I may understand better my own inescapable tendencies
As I consider so many designs beholding
To natural propensities...

Therefore, I do accept that I might break,
I might dissolve, or dry and wither.
I might arrive in surest sorrow,
Or lose the magnificence of my masculine heart.
I do establish that some great part of me may truly fail to survive
If I misjudge to presume that I can make this life
A better dance without her.

Sonnet 84

Where courage will take us,
What sacrifices must, for everlasting love?
What of our strength in hands and open hearts
May hold it carefully?
Sworn to the delight of one another's eyes...

I Have Looked to the River
Which Washes Away the Peaceful Shores

I have looked to the river which washes away the peaceful shores,
My species flows through it in its thrust of flowing insanity.
Our children stand too closely to the left and to the right,
But they have no exclusive clarity to avoid their own drowning.

Predominant in all the river's powerful undercurrents
Is the horror that not one reality of individual perception
Holds any firm anchor into bedrock truth.
No, it isn't your "God,"
No, it isn't your "Party,"
No, it isn't your "Victimhood,"
No, it isn't your "Moral Righteousness,"
No, it isn't your "Sad and pathetic concern,"
No, it isn't your "Journalistic Elitism,"
No, it isn't your "Heavy-handed Government,"
No, it isn't your "Apocalyptic weapon in hand…"

The "Truth" can only be the sum total of what is seen flowing by.
The Truth is, we remain this insane river as always,
Into which we also drown again,
Just like all the past fools who washed away…

How do each of us, against our perfectly comfortable insanity,
Learn to step back from our preciously insane perspective?

I Pray My Gifts, Aeternus Possessio

Thank you, Infinite Lord, for what I am.
I pray you a promise to set me loose into the annealing sun.
Set me free into the bloating sails of what greatness passes away,
For what alien greatness I may yet become,
As I meet dread to forsake my every fortune.

Promise me these of my blessings will not decay asunder:
That I may hold to the primal of musical exultation,
Hold to a radical prose wrote with transcendent invocation,
Hold to the piercingly poignant of deep, emotional attestation,
And for indomitable love kept preserved in its perfect space,
Which heats immortal embers.
Dispossess me not, these my visceral facilities.
For which I become nothing more, the blowing dust,
If beyond this mortal moment, I shall be razed ghostly without…

Ways of Love, Friday's Daydream

How I live to see you again,
Diamonds and sweet vanilla lotion,
A candy glow with sprinkles of glitter…

Come pull me nearer,
Draw me to your approving gaze,
Entangle me now
And make me weaker still,
Within this fever…
I burn through all this day
For your radiant medicine of warm, close fragrance.

I Stand Now More to the Right

With me once, my brothers and sisters…
In the years of Nam and Ohio protest
We were all born to the left.
But those reveries we sang in dreamy innocence
Failed to carry homeward our folksy promises,
As hipster sonnets proclaimed,
For Elysian provinces.
The chords plucked by old left-handed fingers now
Don't ring right from wrong
By virtuous wail of a worn out, spurious song.

Beside me once,
My brothers and sisters countenanced ourselves
The preeminent conspirators,
With ideals garnished in braided flowers,
To make known a new world of utopian powers
Exhorted upon passive bridges of gentler persuasion,
To cross the crevasses of bedeviling predation…
Though as they prove in present tense,
Disingenuous and as typically scurrilous,
Skulks this day's trending partisan predator-species prevailing.

I thought I loved you,
My brother perpetuating with me together, our homeland.
I thought I loved her too,
My sister perpetuating with me together, our homeland.
But you deny me legitimacy of perspective
From my window's pain,
You tell me by intolerant rebuke that I must refrain
As I speak to treachery coming upon us from the yard.

You indict me, and with deaf disregard,
To assail my devotions as evil-natured, nationalist choices.
Though in consequence to these falsities,
These aspersions lain over forcefully muted voices,
This fortress, with its defenses for freedom in community,
Shifts from sound foundation into gradual disassembly.

I stand now more to the right,
As I make preservation of American spaces raised squarely true
Built up by the blisters and the pledges of our mothers and fathers.
I will take refuge outdoors when the roof finally falls through,
I will make camp beside grandmothers' gravesites
While flashes of thunder and harsh light see new storms reign.

And that I may droop wearily in what will become
A terrible and restless night,
I will lean in upon the eroding headstones
Of our greatest grandfathers,
To take my leave for cover and comfort
Sleeping there beneath long, moon shadows casting
From elder monuments with patriotic alters.

Fear me there, that I shall wait and hold out in seclusion.
But never shall I fully arrest,
Nor shall I permanently and invisibly comply
With these liars or their hypocrites and their neo-carpetbaggers
Whom my impolitic brothers and sisters have enjoined to erect
A deleterious mansion of dark labyrinth and dungeons,
Where once did sleep safely our pedigree, our lineage,
Our young, multi-wonderful generation
Of wealthiest liberties imbued.

Beautiful Monique, I Have Lost

Where fairest beauty, of gentle form, of thoughtful poetry,
Composed by delight of her feminine inspiration;
As even the poet's pen cannot write,
As the artist's keen eye may still not quite define it.
Colors of perfect complexion,
Fade – though as sharply as they may be so perfectly blended –
But not enough against the contrast of her glimmering hues
Of golden soul.

Still, I cannot find her, for I am blind and in the dark;
Confused by my dull fingers searching
Too far into misdirected dimensions.
And she will thrive in the warm sunlight,
Bright and beautiful as the eternal day's own grand effort,
While I have diminished into black corners, shriveled and gone.
For adoration's promising path I could not find,
And save me the way out to love's great brilliance
In kindly radiance upon me
From her ineffable, preciously special gaze.

I will not forget her,
Here in my own cavern of shadows.

Memorial to Sutherland Springs, and Las Vegas 2017

Evil's surreal,
Where baby's breath abates hushed in abrupt, stark agony;
A tinge of deathly copper's taste upon the last, unimaginable gasp.
Your horror let loose with weapon raised and braced,
Then I will damn sure strike back at you!

A pock of perception separating Oneness into strangers,
And again into meaningless targets,
As perceived within your sad, mad cerebrum lost.
While the one master's quarks and neutrinos rush straight through,
Only this the tiniest of debris to be left untouched
By the whole heartbreak of human delusion.

Many Kisses for Catherine

Lonesomeness is the mud holding to everyone
While we reach from entrenched ankles to outstretched fingertips,
Reaching to free ourselves upward toward a rising sun.

Sinking in the lonesome mud, everyone…
This hopeless crowd,
Insular hearts too desperately proud,
Needful hands but arms withdrawn, no clasping palms,
Where joys of companionship could arise in passions meld
Then less our lonesome hands through sharing held.
Though instead we stay the stuck beside,
Him and her, you and I.

Yes, we cry betwixt our cohort lonesome,
Cramped between inmates maudlin,
Alike in self-pity to leave us rotten in this surrounding, sinking mud,
Straining our thighs against the consuming, solus crud,
Reaching from entrenched hips to outstretched fingertips
For brightest brilliance higher above
While here we squirm steeper into deeper separation
Though all the world beside us,
In wishful rescue for once true love.

For Socrates

"Nothing comes from its own."
This truth, when misunderstood, appears asunder,
And seems biding in blinded consequence.

Emancipated from embodiment,
From subjective prejudice,
First is the enactment of 'Divine volition,'
Manifest in universal prosperity;
Relevant to all who dwell this infinite domain…

But fabric and stone mislead,
The senses become deluded;
Imagery dissolves the essence
And leads belief
To distinguish Life as many things
Alone
And concluded.

Just a Veil Between Us

Just a veil between us now...
Today I am nearer than breath,
And real as breath unseen.
Dear lover, friend, mortal angel who comforted me,
Find me now beyond the narrow senses
Of human perception.
Living hands stretching out to clasp
Must, in time, release each hand once held.
As we shared so tightly embraced,
Even now, forever you and I adjoin
In heart and soul.

This day that is bright
With the sight of adoring, dutiful lovers,
Is also our light.
Do not deny me, look beyond the painful reflective glare.
Know that I am there,
Growing brighter in your heart and soul.

Sweet as a child's bedtime tales
Our days and nights were spun as classics told,
We two enraptured characters indulged
In Life's richest experiences,
And with the delight of timeless pretenses.
But a truer permanent nucleus arrives
From this interplay of two loving mortals covalent together,
The ageless Truth of us
Is weaved in heart and soul.

I am, you are…
In our togetherness and always as we were separate,
The tide of Time moves us upon a forward wave.
Tomorrow's grand promise
Cannot promise but one day,
While all the world spins to rearrange.
What proof to provide that we are evermore?
But the spirited heart and soul.

By bone and flesh our sentience to attest
This World of opposites;
Joy and sorrow, bliss and despair.
On Earth, human tears have washed mighty mountains
Into the oceans.
This life of love, and equal loss
Presents its paradox
Of rainbows against the rain.
How else can life and love and dreams become,
If not with heart and soul.

My dearest Love,
By strength of faith,
Call to me through the inner veil.
Prepare then, for the warmth of my revealing.
With your smiling face that weeps its tears,
With rainbows and rain,
Take hold this pleasurable pain.
Then speak softly, "Yes, he has come."
Speak softly, "Yes, she has come."
My Love, I will burn brightly
Against your heart and soul.

Special

Like an oasis beyond the hot sands
Like a high note above the bottom grumble
Like a sapphire atop the brown clay
Like a wonder rising from the typical
Like a promise diluting despair
Like a familiar face among the many strangers,

SPECIAL ... she seems to be.

Rage-Thoughts Do Welt the Bodies Human By Madness of Mind

My madness begins
Where I thought, perhaps,
I could peel off these various scabs,
Gold gilded lesions too itchy that won't scrape away.

My madness as rage-thoughts welted upon my extremities,
Seborrheic cankers plump and rounded in their definition…
Was I dis-eased to become this mad human from the start?

The other ill patients and I wept together,
But angrily we resisted one another,
Retreating to the glum, dark corners
Where each of us believed a better chance to survive there alone.
We could have healed in huddles together,
Standing naked at the windows in the warm sunlight
If not for all the dense, obscuring curtains kept fully drawn.

I see the fat lesions grown out on your extremities too,
Rage-thoughts welting up, also from the deep madness in you!

I Break In Two

I break in two because of you.
I've been strong but now I'm weak
Taken to kneel, by your touch to my cheek.
I'm falling or I'm flying
In a space without a floor,
Just to hold you burns inside me
But it scares me so much more
When I feel that I am not the one
You will choose to settle for.

I break in two where my frailty fights for you.
Stranded with imperfections you've come to see,
I'm shaken by these the reasons
You might finally turn from me,
Yet I am enslaved to see it through
While my core of confidence softens at the risk of you.

I break in two by quicksilver desire.
I feel I'm running some tunnel of fire,
While all these affects you've come to enflame
Meld into one lingering focus,
Forged from the two of me and you.

Briefly, like Twilight's Fireflies

Aloft the bluer shades this side the blackest shadows cast,
Opposite the beaming, whitest sun;
We glow there hovering in the temperate, thinner balance,
We strike out our choices, in rare chance to explore.

Between the positive and negative polar extremes,
We blind, bleed.
Painfully, it goes – this hotter glow.
Though briefly, but freely, our joyous flight like twilight's fireflies!

This is Me, While I Breathe

Come before me,
My breath, my visceral life,
My central identity enveloping,
Known to no other,
My quiet current upon which rises
The splashing waves
I know myself to be.
I enfold inseparable reflection
While I breathe,
While I breathe.

This is me,
Where the known universe exists.
This is me,
All that I can say of any truth persists.
I hear the blood flowing,
I feel it as this one being alive,
My own inseparable unanimity
While I breathe,
While I breathe.

Proclaim to me, my lone birth,
I am the tap root extending outward,
None other to know me as my own uprising,
My own deliverance,
My own Earth and Heaven and Hell
While I breathe,
While I breathe.

Where ancient faith and meddling science fails,
My wisp of divine indomitability prevails.
My inner voice speaks all-affirming,
This "me" that I behold as witness confirming,
What magnitude of miracle might I discover?
More of any greater depth but my own existent wonder...
And such it is for you – this Truth – as for all others,
While we breathe,
While we breathe.

Our Sweet Maiden Bronze

I do see a mighty truth, this woman beautiful!
My eye set in awe for her deep Nairobian ebony,
Her fairness in Tahitian pearl,
She is the origin of my world,
My lover or my bosom mother,
The richness of qualities human,
Statuesque in bronze.
Adorned with deep surahs of bold complexion,
She is the radiant, uzuri black!

In this most perfect granddaughter
Continues the grace of the ancient grandmother,
Heavy laden with all these generations
Birthed afar from Ethiopia's womb,
She is mother to all my children beautifully black.

I have witnessed in her a pearlescent pleasance, indelibly sworn,
Her immunity to all the harsh, white winters come and gone.
She praises her babies' finer lives
While she sings to me a quiet cry,
But a cool and kindly lullaby,
A forgiving lyric in sweet prose for better times,
Better inside the refinished rooms of this older home
Where she endured, ever too long estranged.

I see her ferocity of stride across a dark world
While she presents aglow with soft, silken quality,
Ever so strong but tenderly moving, swaying,
As to teach the breezes a supple patience of yielding,
But never breaking…

I embrace her into my arms with all affection,
Rest here upon my shoulder, I beg of her,
Our sweet maiden bronze,
My exquisite angel of the black seed,
Perfect sister in whom all vivacity is so decently human.
Forever the venerable matriarch to all our pristine children
In shades of ebony born.

Monuments as Static Perches for Pigeons

The idolatry or obliteration of symbolic artifacts
Is human deference misplaced;
Time in waste against the precious, brief span of breathing, eating,
Toiling, mating, aging, and dying.
Despite the uproar from all who declare,
 – With egocentric righteousness –
The mightiness of their own personal angst,
Their mythological stones or steeples or bronzes
Will surely always fade in relevance to the far-off descendants;
Shall become truest as stained, static perches for pigeons.

Deference to one another, egos that diminish,
Listening more than speaking…
These are the statuesque characteristics that will one day
Stand revered, never to tarnish.
Stone and steeple and bronze serve to guide us,
But also to blind us along our way there.

Grief Cannot Serve You

Grief cannot serve you,
Nor does it serve those departed.
Walk happily beside that sense of loss,
Even with all its heartfelt abusiveness.
This serves you and your cherished loved ones best
Along our march through time.
Time marching, possesses us. But we possess the timeless past.

Guiding Us, Great Covenant, Brightly!

Wrest your independent mind away from this particular muckraker,
My role played with contempt as one adrift sailor.
Out across seas of distressful swirls,
My trepidation invites me for truthful pearls, and so I dive.

Make no meaning of it,
My barge unmoored for nautical hypotheses,
My cargo of analytical fallacies,
Dredged from the waters, saturated presumptions tease a shine.
But these bright inferences in ephemeral reflections glossed,
Are fleetingly translucent as a certain glare be tossed;
Stippled by the inscrutable undercurrents
Which vex beneath from broad caverns in complex regions.

…Upheaving swells foretell the deep
Which demoralized society cannot tread,
So goes off shore many more the muckrakers and scrutinizers
– Much like me,
Scavenging apprehensively downward into the muck
And the cold dread.

We submerge to uncover,
To unfurl refractions fully,
To reclaim truth from evidentiary artifacts reconstituted.
But these delicate traces hold together in steady shallows only;
Gripped asunder and swallowed into disturbances arching deeper
Imperiled clarity gets crisscrossed again, sinking from us, diluted.

By what aligning sun,
Great star in its eminent orbit
Reveals its mandamus glow before every citizen's bleary eye,
Inculcating us by divine and astral proclamation?
While ascending into its zenith high,
Many desperate and disparate vantage coordinates
– All whom do trim their sails abiding this central beacon guiding –
Become saved ships surfing together;
A fleet on course to one destination.
Following ribbons trailing
In streams brilliant with red and blue lumens bright
Lost mariners find their course again in the sky's liquid night.

By guidance of what astrological body to save us?
But the one extraordinarily rare,
Spun between three moons residing,
There, the small galaxy of fifty as one shining!
As a beam of lighthouse ray white hot with its pull,
As our prescient gull, which leads us best
By gentle glide across the crest;
To stake for us a safe reunion homebound.
Returning to our maiden port and beloved sovereignty,
We fellows and relatives reacquaint there once again,
Steady and stalwart now to our founding covenant betrothed;
From lost, seafaring legs to firmer footing on granite
And hallowed ground:
These expansive plains of unanimity, these rich veins of equality,
And millions the home hearths hewn
From elder forests plenty, of towering deciduous liberty!

Jessi's Poem

I looked upon the face of an angel today...
She glows in the youthful artistry of twenty four years.
With a songlight in her fresh gaze,
She makes me so in love.
She is the young woman's soft, supple, but pert complexion,
Radiant with the brightest in delightful beauty!

I dream to touch her,
To kiss her warm, wonderful cheek.
Possessing the crystal eyes of a perfect feminine masterpiece,
Jessi lulls my heart into a yearning
For all that was once virile, masculine, and young in my life.

If I could be her lover,
Oh, that I could be the passionate hand upon her...
In form, her smooth, toned arms fixate my concentration.
I hunger to kiss Jessi, to caress her,
To hold Jessi with fast-pressed embrace.
Her young twenty four is more delight
Than I will ever know to hold again.

Jessi's translucent shades of highlighted frost,
Which stream and cross
In long, full strands of golden, shimmering hair,
Race into me like sunny beams,
Piercing through the visual pores of my lustful senses,
Heating me deeply with writhing desire!
Her every aspect in form and figure touts the feminine cradle
That I would lay in cover, for soothing, peaceful, bliss.

How I must concede with lonesome certainty,
That I am not a man for her,
For Jessi is but twenty four.
In this, my midlife, I cannot hope to know her
But in the cold of fantasy…

Therein, only might I pretend to kiss… kiss her,
To rest my exhale upon the fold of her mild grin,
Or pretend to nuzzle my lips
Against the vibrant heat of her young, perfect palm.

Continuing in this pale pretense,
I would stir my voice to an ardent whisper
Alighted into the delicate hollow of Jessi's sparkle-studded ear;
While my errant, ageless soul – beleaguered in this aging skin –
Would announce a virgin boy's jittery notion,
A young man's prime and masculine intention,
A wishful senior's ravenous plea,
For the receiving of her warm, young, heaven…

Softly... Of Largo Tempo

Softly... Softly...
Of largo tempo slowly paced,
Patiently taps along as a quiet tick, tock...
Penetrates a charcoal night's opaque silence,
By stroke of pendulum at each pause,
Another faintly clunk knocked aloft
From old Grandfather's coffin cabinet.

While a demure, random drip softly... softly splashes out of sync,
To politely accompany there, though subdued beneath
Like a rain drop patter
Fallen into the earth with a rush of stolen breath.
Steady clepsydra and chronograph nearly so faint
As the early hours' vast, unblemished canvas.

Low, those blunted commands of time,
Heard to perforate with unhurried rudiment of flattened tone.
As will the embalming night's replenishing hold
Hear softly, inside host caverns of quieted dreams,
A patience tapping;
With drowsy stride... a slowness to heel in ghostly clicks,
The soul's atemporal strolling across graveyard bricks.

In God's Image Eternal

God stares not down upon me
God shares my every breath.
God is not my awaiting judge,
God is my soft-spoken mentor within.

And when death takes my last hungry breath away,
God is not my resting soul's final keeper.

God is instead the spirited, resurgent life
Expressing forth as all the manifest realm.
Into God, by death my singularity resolves.
Then upon God,
By birth I am thrust to embody once more.

I breathe and express anew,
While God delights within creation.
God's heart is my heart,
One lifetime onto another,
Ever flowing as rising and receding tides eternal.

This Rancor in Me, Angry American

Burdened by brash liars stacking up like dominos clacking on,
Deflated and flattened upon my back
From rued personal dramas of instances long gone,
And ripening age erodes grasp of my conciliatory, poetic heart.
Puttering about neither backward nor beyond
Is just ill-fate of frozen mood.

Conquests for suitable serenity seem just too high upon the shelf.
Attempting to overlook deceit or fraud or evil political doers,
Rocks me unsteadily like stretching high from a three leg stool.
No use to cede anti-American, apathetic fool...

Over the secluded nighttime, indignant hermit neocon
Broods through the spyglass true, into riot fires
Lit by torches thrown by hypocrite race-baiting liars.
Inside me a writhing war against all that's degenerating
From this practical home I naively once supposed.

In this second civil war's lonesome trench,
I daydream a reckoning march of armies reclaiming,
If only I could see rise on the battlefield Arlington,
The reincarnating Eisenhower, Grant, Washington!
Best perhaps that elder, lonesome grunts like me
Cast off hopes for late love and serenity;
Run instead to emancipate the socialist congressional halls,
Or subside into mortar craters nearby El Paso walls.

From all this that stirs me provocative in mind,
Affixed to each sunrise, new broadcasts of fresh lies;
Low sadly, I still dream deeply of sweet touch and kisses
And conversation,
My darling rare will however surpass me by.
Rather would she, a less concerned gentleman
Preening his disposition brighter.
And no good woman then of amicable heart could tolerate
As I may suffer,
This rancor in me would soon unrest my demure lover,
For what I – innate loyal citizen – cannot help to decry!
I stand alone then, angry American...

Yes! To All His Best!

In the sad, past gloom,
No soul lingers to be there memorialized…

The wind sweeps smooth, signs of yesterday's tussle in the dirt.
The host of ghostly spirits does not linger to mourn
For once-animate creation fallen down to fade.

Take your memories as a better guidepost to understand
And to appreciate this day's new dawn.
For even the ill-fallen have left old claims behind
To forge new beginnings onward.

Richer now do we become,
To remember them each new day by their gifts to us in glory!

Yes! To all his best, my Todd Ingle!

Perfect Woman, Do Love Thyself

By great measure of a woman's tender miracles, defines her;
Where the infinite father imbues her to be naturally perfect
In her effortless love.
But how she forgets,
As she cannot see
Her own beautiful presence of expressive generosity,
Her invaluable compassion.
Blind for a moment she might be,
While I can see her clearly to embody all that is love, truly.

Swans of Noble Monogamy

Not like you or I,
The Swans instead glide higher
To further heights of Loyalty,
Where Love is the companion
Taken to flight beside,
With no truer course
But the flight taken together.

For monogamous swans by two,
His flight is her presence,
As his presence is flight for her,
Content to be transient
In the quiet, coolness
Of their home aloft...
Love is this, their familiar wing
Sharing one course,
Toward indeterminable destination.

How each cares enough
To land together,
Splashing down together,
Hunting each day's food as two beside,
So this be the Love in two mated swans,
And no greater in Human beings
Could we impart to one another
Sweeter heights, nor truer flights
Into love aloft...

But as fate will always do, Life and time for Love
Slip beneath us fast.
For all great Love, a dowry will be taken
In final loss and separation.
Once where two swans roamed,
Now one left alone, circling in his rings of loss,
Fading to become half the bird
By her endless absence.

The beautiful white swan
Quietly succumbs to be a lesser bird,
While transient Flight is given up
To the past.
A noble patience our swan suffers
For the dying day,
This the quiet bird adorns upon himself
With a delicate majesty,
Like that of his brilliant plumage.

As once a great bird of the air,
No more the spirited flight in this cobbled wing,
For the breadth of Swan's loss.
Her brilliant mated swan
Now becomes a tender duck
Piddling about around his pond,
Lost in his ever-waiting
For the return of her fair feather.

For Love in One Reflected

In the world she speaks,
She moves as the woman.
She is my mother, my lover, the parent soul...
I am the father, her lover;
Her innocent boyish reflection,
Drawn up from the divine.
I am the one who waits to join her...

I move as one in the masculine,
To find myself in the one who
Moves as feminine.
Then sweet separate souls can blend again
To be the one love whom is whole...
My mother, my father.
My mind, my soul.
My lover and I.

Twenty Four Frail Mice

There is a little mouse living outside my house,
So frail and tiny against the rage outside,
Always looking for somewhere to hide.
Must I, with a heart of gold, welcome this tiny mouse?
"Please, come live inside my house."

Here the harmless, soft creature has taken its refuge with me,
Scampering about, a few black pellets dropped throughout.
I am keen to spot them and remove them for my little guest.

Soon enough during the harsh winter's freezing blow,
Comes my little guest's brethren shivering at my door.
I count them: one, two, just a few.
And as they scurry along within where I take my sleep,
Outdoors, a pathway through the dark, cold night has been plotted
For many desperate more.

As I awake to find them, what should I do?
Must I let twenty more nearly frozen creatures in?
And this I do again.
Twenty shivering, frail mice huddled at my door,
Weakly stumble through.

I share my bread,
I keep the fire stoked against the raging storms outside.
Twenty four warm mice busy themselves,
Coming and going from nests where they hide.

Time passes,
And I have come to notice my warm shelter was never enough.
Twenty four guests have scurried themselves
And their tiny, black droppings all through my stuff.

While I sleep, they venture deep into my cabinets,
Leaving behind unhealthy disturbances
Caused by their innocent mice habits!
The bread and crumbs needed to feed
Will not last as long,
To keep my guests and myself alive, I must go more often.
Exposed to the bitter weather,
Now I must suffer the storms outside my shelter.

I identify with praise for my own golden heart,
My kind reasoning, my generosity to impart.
But I am feeling ill now for all the ways inhospitable to me,
Living amongst the mess of frail mice and their flea.
I consider it laudable, these troubles endured for twenty four,
Although the storms of yesterday continue today,
And now there are two hundred ten desperate, shivering mice
Scratching away my door!

Alone in my home, with its din and disease,
The storm has found its way to me
Through the mice and their fleas.
Cute as the frail, innocent mice might be,
Forlorn as they will always remain,
I am here withering with disease just the same.
I am a frail, shivering human
Stricken by my own golden heart,
For all the empathy I would hold,
And guilt for storms I did not start.

Would I have been better for,
The twenty four left dead outside my door?
Even so, I did not save two hundred ten
Against the storms that always rage from earthly nature
Or nature evil set loose in men.

In my cries, I plead to a mystery I did not design!
Am I a fool to make my charity by some small part,
To self-sooth in just one virtuous heart?
I watch as drowned mice, drowned babies, dreams of peace
Float lost in sink holes below the storms.

I cry from guilt while I exterminate those frail mice of twenty four,
My health, my life is also right to defend.
I too will scratch down every door before my end.
In my guilty cries, I plead to a mystery I did not design!
Culpable that I am, guilty by my innocent witness
To the infirmities always a pox upon the sweet sublime…
One more unsettling paradox in express, a turbulent rhyme.

Ways of Love, Friday's Sunset

Resonant reminiscence,
A plague of hallowed echoes through my heart,
My lost lover's voice drifts across precious images,
A tearful haunt, overcast in treasured rainbows too;

With the memory's end, a sunny brightness breaks through,
And I reclaim once again how much I'll always love you...

All the Dogs Barkin' For Sweet Sharon Clarkin

All the dogs are up and barkin,
Excited to sense the homeward Clarkin.
Sharon entices by the sweet scent,
A pollen drift she brushes aloft
From the crimson petals of her delicate rose.

All her puppies with their love for her,
Come rushing home to surround her bed,
To keep safe Sharon's quiet bloom of sweet repose.

My Idol, My Wonder, Lust and Love

In this world of women,
This sea of delicately artful creatures,
I cannot help but to adore them greater
Than all other beauty everywhere.
What am I to do?
When even the sight of two small, pellucid buttons – low cut
In soft, pastel cotton dimpled over a hidden cleavage,
Enthralls my eye to imagine, to sense the warm,
Bosom creamy beneath;
Which allures and charms like a peaceful pillow,
Precious enough to rest my cheek in perfect comfort.

Women destine me to live each day in want, insatiable desire,
For their hair, perfume, eyes, tender complexion,
Torsos of feminine beauty;
To the buxom,
To the petite,
To the curvaceous,
To the lean and muscular torsos,
To the rotund and supple torsos;
All of them in their glory
Parading each as beautiful women before me,
Beaming into me like heat rays of photosynthesis
For the green, masculine bloom.
I am a helpless flower, a rooted stalk dependent,
Coupled to Eve's enormous radiance!

This solar sea of women
Which defines my only life, my orbit, my pain, my pleasure,
And absolutely my only real purpose.
To embrace her.
To enfold her perfect power.
To witness her as the one noble and worthy value
In this whole disturbing life.

Where Rogues Take Away,
Rangers Will Fight to Retrieve

Two brothers face off, ready for war.
Evil Kane and goodness Abel...
Always the same as then before.

Unavailing Conservative patriarchs
Against inutile Marxist matriarchs:
Plea, "Repudiation at the pulpit!" they wail...
Though less for any meaningful resolve it captures,
But more their glory in obstinate statures.
Soon, angry constituents will rise
With their own weapons brought to the fight,
Kane and Abel, both wrong or both right.
Somehow our foundational principles relinquish – forsaken,
And anarchists do throng... over the long, murderous night.

Provocative legislators, as always, rush for refuge
Inside safer, privileged halls,
While a necessary and critical profundity stalls,
In waste of capably logical reasoning.
And a blanching flag will suffer its deep blue fading,
Its arteries of sacred red, slowly... mortally drained.
The hypocrisy of the rogue autocracy will falsify
For commissions to indict those patriots wrongfully blamed.

These rage affairs which plague to reoccur,
Condemn the young Kane and Abel marching conscripted
Onto bone fields
Where Yankees and Rebels, heroes and devils, foes and friendlies,
Have all feared in dread,
Fresh terror brought again as chaos among brothers,
Hemorrhage the sadness such as biblical Kane and Abel bled.

…This time, not for enslavement eradicated,
Not for a noble Republic Constitutionally united,
This ensuing malice grows
From the gross deeds of whom are the malicious!
Where evil Kane and evil Abel, for power lust,
Prey all their lies upon us;
Where each transgresses upon the other,
Enriching themselves by contract
For professional snipes, acrimonious.

I say, "Let there be War!"
Enrage us as this defensive violence in Kane and Abel!
Ready us to kill the evil as always goodness has killed it before!
Where rogues take away, rangers will fight to retrieve!
Allow vast death to ensconce which reality shall then prevail,
Whatever destiny; surviving only as victors achieve.

God is a murdering warrior in the archetypal soldier for Humanity.
Thereby goes the poor mortal price we pay in fragile Kane and Abel
To pay Divine Kartikeya's wage in bloody sacrifice;
Because grim wars beset upon the evil immoral
Must in rescue, forever tenuous tranquility.

Paradox Two

Paradox will find you
Where the opposite amplitudes intersect.

A place of helical reality
Both in positive and negative,
And for the realities of Love and Hatefulness.

At the equilibrium,
Hope and Despair are freely the crosscurrents
Where free will is yours' to explore.

Ann in the Beautiful Dunes of My Time

Just as our wind-swept love,
We felt all the swirling, sandy grains.
A cool sunny lit day,
A stinging rush of pinging pleasures, pains,
Raptures of soft high banks,
With brief memories in difficult footsteps,
Rinsed away in the sandy winds.

While we arrived there,
To gaze in wonder at vast panoramas of rolling peaks on high,
To share precious, precious moments,
You and I... and our quiet, four-legged friend,
This was our family,
There in the swirling winds.
Kindly, carefully, gently,
Preserving a timeless moment,
Upon a beautiful, ever-rearranging dune.

Precious Pulse Intrinsic to the Whole

Beating within this chest,
The isolated heart, the lonesome breath…
Eyes that perceive the world around
As desperate depth.

And we yearn to reach out, to brush against
One warm, soft finger,
While our night's lonesome visions
Get cast against silent walls surrounding;
Wail the tale of our quiet loss
In a room alone.

So pray this meditation unending until we feel its truth:
We are integral breath and inseparable pulse
Tethered to six billion plus;
Each a living heart hopelessly singular, and fabulously intrinsic
To the collective whole of us…

Real

'Real'
Can be places,
Can be anything,
Must be…
It cannot avoid manifestation.

'Real sunlight'
Emitting shapes and shadows
Through our minds,
Is spectacular,
Its brilliance and brightness!

Mostly,
In the land of 'Real,'
Are sounds:
Roaring along the air…
And a needle whispering,
Clattering upon the floor.

Starlight Myrna

Myrna,
Like a fallen, innocent mockingbird,
My beautiful ghost,
If I could have recovered you...
No greater beauty in all my years of searching
Have I found here,
No woman prettier could I hope to hold in my arms.
Brunette wonder,
Blue eyes deep as pools,
So alike these clearest, glacial waters
Where you rest nearly beyond.

Myrna,
Princess of rising stardom, there with your two princess baby girls,
Fatefully taken to flight at the day
A loyal audience in love
Would cherish to retain you.
All the sorrows frozen,
Rigid in sad glaciers,
Wept a frost in crystal tears to behold you.
A rare, warm flower blown in on a cold, cruel wind,
Misplaced beauty lost in a desolate world.
Arrested beneath these violent boulders,
Thrust from us, your innocent heart.
Your youthful magic forsaken,
Against a tragic slope.

I could have loved you,
In sweet lips of kisses,
Had destiny rearranged your seasons
To run beside me.
I am here upon this harsh cliff today
Reaching out to fall into your eyes,
With all their sky blue,
Veiled now behind the wispy clouds.
And I shout loudly to towering mountain walls,
"Myrna, elegant Myrna,
With your baby girls!"
Feel me near your solemn grave,
I am here at the summit
With all my empathy pounding,
For aloft was lost sweet Myrna and her tragic darlings.

We come to remember,
The babies, the boys, the mother and men,
Eight precious souls to follow this new angel through.
Prettiest angel, risen to become Heaven's wing of finest feather,
Myrna's lovely grace, here with us forever.
Murmured amongst these cliffs
Our prayers, in quiet, respectful echoes,
"Myrna, Myrna Ross…"

Golden Mother Shining

Into the night's cool silence
My heartbeat resonates;
A murmur of slow passage flows forward
In deep currents toward the dawn.

Babies not seen, are heard
Through quietly concerning echoes
Where heart strings hold to them tightly,
From the cradle's distance drawn closer
By my greatest love.

I will see to it that the next dawn comes,
Because I will hold to my babies
In no weaker a faith than this as mine to command.
I am their mother,
I burn for them, endless in my resolution,
White hot forever
With my maternal fusion shining.

Username... Password...

I'm sitting here looking at photos of you,
I spend my days sifting profiles too!
I'm stuck on dating sites to find my life,
I'm lost on the internet to find my wife!

I'm flipping through blondes to brunettes, hair long to short,
Asian, Black, White or Latino lovers of every sort!
Today's dance for romance swings on a Smartphone screen,
She's there, she's gone... Two days texting don't mean anything!
I keep forgetting to pay my bills,
I traded off fishing, hiking, and outdoor thrills
To sit at home and agonize through computer skills!

She boasts to be a Humanist, devoted to the starving poor,
I'm a Constitutionalist with my bad-ass weapon beside the door!
She wants to travel Tutankhamun's tomb,
My wishful adventure is a nightly romance in a dim lit room!

Moving on then, to another internet lover!

User name...
Password...
Username...
Password...

No Nest to Rest

Lost,
I wander this life of empty days
Like a bird cast away
Out over the lonesome ocean blue
Where there is no nest to rest.
A sentient, solicitous heart which beats
To need, to share, to empathize, to caress, to encourage,
Has found no place for folding weary wings,
Adrift above this undulating fate...
In flight then, always alone.

Ways of Love, Saturday's Quiescence

Again and again,
I say, "Hold me,
Hold me within you!"

Be you sweet woman,
…Planet,
…Or universe.

And after you have loved me,
Bring my ocean to a calm.

We Percuss Our Inborn Chord

Our dear Lord will blossom gardens endless with fine flowers,
Her creatures crawling, and brilliant stars will all prove beautiful!
A sanctity of great gift born within each of us,
We are the Lord's perfect fruit.

In each of every manifestation,
Artistry infused with animation, and for nothing more but,
A Creator's playful intercourse between God and God's creation.

His divine genius, a resolute force impassioned to conceive us,
A Composer composing while he plays
To each of one and everything,
At once serenading, yet singing within and through…

We notes phrased into chiming melodies ringing,
We notes striking out with high frenzied energies beaming,
We bellows heavy in droning chorus
Before hushing into gravity's arresting silence,
While her schemes, paced in dramatic tempo, portend all orbits go
Along ledgers of Time and Space.

We percuss our inborn chord,
Contributing to atone our thankful, burning gift
As best we play our rare, exclusive music
Beside birth and life and death,
And we accompany all that is high, all that is low,
What is light and what is dark,
The reign of all voices coalesced in universal sonnet,
To resound his symphony dreamed astral,
Finally, for all to blend a philharmonic ethereal.

For it is our composer's position of focus,
Verily nigh though aloft transcendent,
To enjoy alone this wholeness in Harmony.

Across in the garden where her finest flowers bloom,
Three perennial instruments undertake his mythic croon.
A Trio of body, mind, and spirit
Sustain one deep chord breezy but thundering
Of one leading tone strident from your wellspring driven,
Beside one key note you utter in a whimper of wondering,
Reciting Life's discordant song moving along
Mysteriously, in diametric composition, this eternal play.

Devil Unto Myself

I am the devil unto myself,
I am the brutal pirate set to scuttle my own ship,
I am once the value of a good man,
Now discounted worthless.

Where I once could give,
And give dependably for love's great sake,
I have no character left in me to shoulder love's burden…

I am sick and free now in a barren life of my own withdrawn design.

Death by the Legislators' Swords

If I stand tomorrow, ready to take you down,
My weapon aimed straight ahead,
To defend this homeland
Where stolen Constitution torn in raped liberties,
And its many defending, sacrificed lives lain.

Am I in sin to blame?
More the multitude invading marauders,
Come marching lawless with larceny ambition
To sweep me and my babies away…

My own government is the horrible hell
Which stabs me from behind in gory betrayal.
Caesar, we too cry deeply, this death by the Legislators' swords...

Hard Temper upon the Jefferson Anvil

In this our house, our world; in this our home America,
The lawful, the spiritual order of things unfolds in paradox;
This day, tempered steel can become a mighty hardness
Or too brittle against a changing fire:

Paradoxical Order –
Freedom: breeds two children, the virtuous but also the devious;
Time: too long in coming about, but passing by too quickly;
Evolution: the joy of adaptation, but the agony of mutation;
Individuality: self-awareness, but isolation;
Possession: wealth, but poverty;
Faith: community, but rivalry.
Wisdom whispers,
Folly roars,
…And on and on we observe the American opposites exemplified.
Strong men and weak men malign,
Where the inextricable ironies reside;
Then there remains the Thomas Jefferson,
Of whom transcends a dubious play…

Lies from men are light, and roll easily,
Truths from men are heavy, and slow to roll;
Jeffersonian vision describes a golden leaf, but to a blind audience.
Jeffersonian life looks like free flight,
Though too much to risk outside our ponderous mesh of safety nets;
American persons are careful and well-meaning,
American people are little more than herds, known to wander.

Confucius was a Jefferson, but in another time
And a land far removed from current day 'Communist China.'
Gandhi as a Jefferson, guided India with compassion and wisdom,
But assassinated then by radical religious infirmities...

Upon a Jeffersonian anvil, America may be re-hammered,
If only her ignorance and apathy within is mere innocence misled,
But if in her people, brittle America is willingly ignorant,
Lazy and indifferent,
Flames will forebode to melt a majestic nation, nevermore...

Doing the wrong thing exacts a short-term, comfortable status quo.
Doing the right thing demands a dredging of honest strength,
Mined clean from a mire of weakness and denial.
Nowhere to be is Jefferson's America,
If we the anemic descendants are weak in patriotic temper,
And in fear of sacrifice.

Seraphic Anna

Throw away God,
No saving grace to be won from drear mythology,
Great ghost harboring no real form of magnificence...
None. There is no wonder of you as faith makers may believe it.
Not in this kingdom has thou come.

But of divine will to be done,
Behold her palpable magnificence instead,
Seraphic, virtuoso lovely, seated upon a piano's bench;
She taps out Rachmaninoff,
Splendorous keys coo of a fair, heavenly and possible dream:
To hold her and to love her.

Erase this strange graphite sunken deep into me,
This deranged, nagging strife,
That pale floss of some abstract host,
Great ghost harboring no real form of magnificence,
But of a lingering torment taught to me at earliest morn,
Beyond a mere fortnight from my attendant purity born,
I can confuse too much about you – my mute, my vacant God.

Although... This dearly charming artist,
Clearly she teaches me right here of heaven's anticipated covenant,
Through chords she's pressing sweetly soft,
Or attacking dramatically aroused,
Storied notes strung aloft impassioned,
Like loosened pearls chased off a swirling, lashing string;
Aloft musically she bares her perfect self before me,
Her emotive musical recitation as evidence, a Goddess into being.

Seraphic Anna, with her moody fingers,
Captivates the quiet, vacant myth of love;
Drawn nearer to her, I let go this frigid, unholy ghostly myth
For tangible adoration far warmer, proven to me in close audience,
Abreast this born apparition with pianissimo fingers whispering;
I too ring out for her, struck as a key upon her bridge,
Won over, I resonate to accompany her with gladly faithful worship.

No, God. Be thrown finally away from me!
There is no wonder of you as faith makers may believe it.
Not in this kingdom has thou come.
But of divine will to be done,
Behold her palpable magnificence instead,
Seated upon a piano's bench;
She taps out Rachmaninoff,
Splendorous keys coo of a fair, heavenly and possible dream:
To know her is but effortless to love her!

Disparate Lovers

As two hearts may interplay
From steep depths of affection and intense attraction,
Therein arises their true lust sworn.

And in their captured love,
Might two lovers become as one heart,
Beating together always…

But what fate for right lust
Alive in two unfortunate lovers,
As two people
Against incompatibilities to separate them more
Than ardent love may unify?

Amative hearts find no refuge to harbor safely,
Inland a surging seawall storm,
Menacing where worn and weary lovers
Toil to coddle incongruous styles
While such becomes their own petulant child.

Holding fast, lovers wrap love carefully.
Spun in hope, dreamt tightly into a frail weave,
Darling disparates raise high their love in delicate weave secure,
However narrowly clear the rippling surface and perilous undertow.

Lovers' travail, of measured duty,
Not like unfailing devotion to infants newly born,
But as devotion indeterminate between amorous partners,
Promises no perpetuity,
And harsher still, as rip tides may reveal
To one day orphan drowning, discordant lovers.

Alone though together,
Awash this unchosen, discordant and dreary Atlantic storm…
A capsize of two, cling tightly the wet splinters
Upon one love-struck bobbling plank waning afloat.
Adrift in mad thirst,
No chance a sip of once sweet spring water shared,
Disparate lovers spin away in their frothy sea of insoluble drift,
Sunken treasures,
And murky fathom.

We, the Survivors

We are the survivors, you and I.
We endure to reach the days of smooth sailing.
We are not swallowed in the stormy seas.
We are the survivors
As we ride out the battering winds.
We are mighty in our strength to hold on.

We are the survivors, you and I.
Ours' is the generation of heroes.
We are not stopped by the losses drawn from us
In desperate pools.
Our children watch in admiration
As our lofty sails grope the slimmest breeze
And deliver us into smoother waters.

We are the survivors,
Bold, embattled,
Undaunted and victorious against each exhausted storm.
It is only the Divine Ocean that will once consume us.

As survivors, we stay to see the sunshine,
We seek out the clear blue sky.
We survive for sunny days that glitter across the water,
Like a bright dusting of emeralds fallen from Heaven.
Delivered again into clear, tepid waters,
We know this as God's praise for us,
We, the survivors…

Feelings from a Photo,
Never a Lie that I Loved Her Truly

I cannot say "no,"
"No, I do not love her…"
I simply try to let her go again,
As I look at her photo, there's a thousand kisses
I still hold for those cheeks and her lovely brow,
But I cannot come back to her now.

I cannot say "there were no good reasons,"
To wave good bye,
But a fire for her still burns inside.
And a lovely photo tells me
Just how deeply I had fallen too,
A lovely photo of a home I loved so, in a perfect smile.

No I cannot tell her…
No good to tell her we were almost there,
But I feel it painfully,
As I gaze here at something special – her in a photo;
I'm feeling full of love that I cannot show,
For all the puzzling pieces that sorted us too,
Still, I am naturally taken to prize each puzzling jewel.

I will never say "no,"
"No, I do not love her…"
I will simply try to let her go,
Each time as I return to behold her in a perfect photo,
I will say "yes,"
"Look my Love, I am here again, yes kissing you."

Immortal Ember

She's in the fire,
Burning away in the night,
Glowing in the absence,
Fighting for her life.

He's mad with determination,
Waiting for a break,
Feels his insignificance
None other than unique.

Capture, contain this
By the night and its stars,
Feel the burning of her fire,
Strain to bear his insignificance.

With all this
And the movement of your own heart,
Retain an understanding;
'Void all else in conclusion,
And steady yourself in the suffering.

Oblivious, continue onward.
Beware beguiling treachery;
Transcend your own pain
And let not the wind
Carry her from you.

She's afire beside him,
In light of him,
Heavy with kinetic ember.
The eyes he has seen
May very well be his own,
At the opening ahead,
Yet far beyond his mortal creature.

Hence then, transformed;
Given in life's name,
His purpose served in open flame.
That he too, may hold the heavy weight of fame
Upon those hands ever so blistered...

And now, if this light in view
Inflames its plight on you,
Will you hesitate, or reconsider?
Don't!
Stand in open flame
Until yours is blistered fame,
And you've a glow of immortal ember.

Immaculate Reflection

Of all these lands stretching across,
And all the worldly seas,
In its orbit of beingness,
Earthbound twirling around for me.

My mother, wed within my father,
Gleaming upon me in golden sunlight
While she entertains me,
A masterful puppeteer gently stringing aloft
Those vast troops of bellowing characters in costume clouds!
I watch easily, laughing,
Enjoying beneath the cool shady shadows he casts upon me
From his gorgeous, generous, magnificent oak.
The moment is one we enjoy together from my human eyes…

We daydream together in lingering thought,
Prance together in adventurous play,
We admire the significance of one another,
In reverence for one another
While his quiet mood whispers across my unburdened heart,
While she and I are satisfied to gaze like two mirrors faced eternal.

This good day, common day, oh holy day,
Deep drink of precious life;
A sweet blessing upon me
For the mere compensation each breath will have me do.
That I embrace the creator into this creation
While I spin the sway and the step of my human expression
To enfold within this dance together,
My creator's symbiosis through.

A Walk, Holding Hands

That's all she wanted was
A man to hold her hand.

So many ways I moved,
Perhaps she didn't understand,
But a warm touch with little more required
Was the deep friendship she desired.

That's all she wanted was
A man to hold her hand.

Where I failed her
So many times over
Was just to take her hand and hold her.
That's all she needed was
A man to hold her hand,
To walk beside, to understand.

Where I failed
So many times, succeeding so few
At simple movements closer,
A touch of hands,
Strolling the simple walks to see her through.

Ways of Love, There Will I Follow

Sooner would I die,
Letting go this grand old life in me reminiscing today,
Chase instead, my love through the final curtains;
Beyond death's cold repercussions…

Give the Lord's fabulous, ghostly wonder
Birth for new feet, into silken hair, into powerful heart!
Let me run again, winning new beginnings rising through,
Racing forward to touch you there,
To rediscover us in a budding springtime fresh,
Romantic, resplendent!

Love is a Pour of Tears

Love is a pour of tears,
A gentle rain not of pain or of fears,
Lo the emotional touch from what cannot be described,
Yet its truest reign, spilling out from the ardent, indivisible heart.

Surge sweetly, my swollen tears as I attend with you,
My glee for rush of glory suffused, such a seeping artesian pour,
I am drawn into, back through your breach overwhelming
To receive the flowing rain,
There, all quiet communion roils with warm,
Glad tears from my eyes.
This is my maker's munificent pouring, swelled into spawn of
My humbled cries;
Our Lord's bliss spilling through my elated pour of tears!
Born to love and to behold my true progenitor for all my years,
Let me come to this deep swell of pouring rain,
Let these seas surge to flood alive my world again.

A pour of tears fallen to quench a world of thirsty plains,
Love's weep sent seeping through to weary roots,
A soak of grace thrust wilted durum once again swaying
With stronger stems blonde in bounteous grains,
And to nourish this hungry shepherd boy beside his baby lamb.

Love is a wailing tidal rising;
Devoted daughter, be carried along,
Devoted son, ride high,
Love's inner resource rushing outward through rolling waves,
Fanning joyous spray;
Let the wailing tidal arise in our tears for great love
As best our deep gratitude we pray.

Always do we buoy in centered waters together,
Centered to a perfectly tepid and calmer eye,
Entrusting our journey into the merciful Poseidon.
Love is a pour of tears,
Of bliss awash and raining,
Swelling up from the deepest artesian, ardent heart;
Wherefrom my presence in you, dear Lord,
Tenders me in warmest pours I cry.

Showers across this world,
We receive all from its bathing, fertile storm,
To quench every seed sown in love for you and for me.
Lo, and while we rest afloat a tepid and calmer eye,
We open to receive love's gentle reign,
As love kisses, timeless eternal, with a pour of tears...

© *This in Words,*
For Reverence of Wonder...

~ *Philip Holland* ~